G000277370

A weekend's worth of *essential* words and phrases

Translated by Athene Chanter

First published in Great Britain in 2002 by
Michael O'Mara Books Limited
9 Lion Yard, Tremadoc Road
London SW4 7NQ

A CIP catalogue record for this book is available from the British Library

ISBN 1-85479-084-6

1 3 5 7 9 10 8 6 4 2

Designed and typeset by Design 23

Made and printed in Great Britain by William Clowes, Beccles, Suffolk

CONTENTS

INTRODUCTION

Concise yet informative, *French to go* is ideal for weekend visits to *la belle France* – a regular glance at the contents of this pocket-sized language book will ensure you'll never be lost for words.

Clear and precise, the pronunciation that follows each French word and phrase has been devised to simplify the French language for the English-speaking user, with the aim of producing more relaxed and flowing conversations with the people you meet.

Make the most of your French adventure with *French to go* – whether you're making a hotel reservation, finding your way to the beach or chatting up the locals, speaking French has never been easier.

NOTE ON PRONUNCIATION: When you see a 'ñ', you should nasalize the vowel before it and not pronounce the 'ñ' itself. For example, 'man' should be pronounced as in the familiar French word 'fin', rather than the English 'man'; 'uñ' should be pronounced as in 'bruñ'; and 'on' as in 'moñ'.

THE BASICS

Hello
Salut
sa'loo

Goodbye
Au revoir
oh ruh'vwar

Good morning
Bonjour
boñ'zhoor

Good afternoon
Bon après-midi
bon ap'ray mee'dee

Good evening
Bonsoir
boñ'swar

Good night
Bonne nuit
bon nwee

Yes
Oui
wee

No
Non
noñ

Please
S'il vous plaît
seel voo play

Thank you
Merci
mehr'see

You're welcome.
Il n'y a pas de quoi
eel nee a pa duh kwah

Thank you very much
Merci beaucoup
mehr'see boh'koo

How are you?
Comment allez-vous? / Ça va?
ko'moñ tallay voo / sa va

Fine / Not bad
Bien / Pas mal
byañ / pa mal

Pleased to meet you
**Je suis heureux(se) de faire votre /
ta connaissance**
*zhuh sweez uhr' ruh(ruhze) duh fehr votr /
ta kon'ay'soñs*

Excuse me
Excusez-moi
eks'koo'zay mwa

Sorry
Désolé(e)
day'sol'ay

Pardon?
Pardon?
par'don

Do you speak English?
Parlez-vous anglais?
par'lay vooz oñ'glay

I don't understand
**Je ne comprends
pas**
*zhuh nuh
koñ'proñ pa*

9

I'm English
Je suis anglais(e)
*zhuh sweez oñ'glay /
(glaze)*

My name is...
Je m'appelle...
zhuh ma'pel...

Could you repeat that more slowly,
please?
**Est-ce que vous pourriez répéter cela
plus lentement s'il vous plait?**
*ess kuh voo poo'ree'ay ray'pay'tay suh'la
ploo lahn'te moñ seel voo play*

Could I pass by?
Est-ce que je pourrais passer?
ess kuh zhuh poo'ray pass'ay

Why?	What?	Who?
Pourquoi?	**Quoi?**	**Qui?**
poor'kwa	*kwa*	*key*

When?
Quand?
koñ

How?
Comment?
ko'moñ

How much / How many?
Combien?
koñ'byañ

Where?
Où?
oo

Which?
Lequel?
luh'kel

Is it far?
Est-ce que c'est loin?
ess kuh say lwañ

Could I have...?
Est-ce que je pourrais avoir...?
ess kuh zhuh poo'rayz av'war

Can you tell me...?
Est-ce que vous pouvez me dire...?
ess kuh voo poo'vay muh deer

Can you help me?
Pouvez-vous m'aider?
poo'vay voo may'day

GETTING FROM A TO B

AIRPORTS & ARRIVALS

Where is / Where are the... ?
Où est / Où sont... ?
oo ay / oo soñ

baggage reclaim
la réception des bagages
la ray'sep'sioñ day bag'azh

luggage trolleys
les chariots à bagages
lay sha'ree'oh a bag'azh

help / information desk
le bureau d'information
luh boo'roh dañ'for'ma'sioñ

ladies' / gents' toilets
les toilettes pour femmes / hommes
lay twa'let poor om / fam

Are there any cash machines here?
Y-a-t-il des distributeurs d'argent ici?
*ee a teel day dees' tree'boo'tuhr
   dar'zhoñ ee'see*

Is there a bureau de change nearby?
Y-a-t-il un bureau de change par ici?
ee a teel uñ boo'roh duh shoñzh par ee'see

Is there a bus / train to the town centre?
Y-a-t-il un bus / train pour aller au centre ville?
ee a teel uñ boos / trañ poor al'ay oh soñtr veel

TAXI!

Is there a taxi rank nearby?
Y-a-t-il une station de taxis par ici?
ee a teel oon stass'ee'oñ duh taxi par ee'see

How much will it cost to get to...?
Combien cela va coûter pour aller jusqu'a...?
koñ'byañ suh'la va koot'ay poor all'ay zhoos'ka

Take me to this address please.
**Emmenez moi à cette adresse, s'il
   vous plaît.**
em'enay mwa a set ad'ress, seel voo play

CAR & BICYCLE HIRE

Where can I hire a car / bicycle?
**Où est-ce que je peux louer une
   voiture / un vélo?**
*oo ess kuh zhuh puh loo'ay oon
   vwa'toor / uñ vay'lo*

I'd like to hire a car for a day / week.
**Je voudrais louer une voiture pour une
   journée / semaine.**
*zhuh voo'dray loo'ay oon vwa'toor poor
   oon zhoor'nay / suh'men*

What is the daily / weekly rate?

Quel est le tarif par jour / par semaine?

kel ay luh ta'reef par zhoor / par suh'men

PUBLIC TRANSPORT

I'd like a single / return to ...

Je voudrais un aller simple / aller retour pour...

zhuh voo'dray uñ all'ay sañ'pl / al'ay ruh'toor poor

What time does the next train / bus to...leave?

A quelle heure part le prochain train / bus pour...?

a kel uhr par luh pro'shañ trañ / boos poor

Which platform does it leave from?
Il part de quel quai?
eel par duh kel kay

Which bus goes to...?
Quel bus va à...?
kel boos va a

Where should I catch the number...bus?
Où est-ce que je peux prendre le bus numéro...?
oo ess kuh zhuh puh proñdr luh boos noo'may'roh

How much is the fare to...?
Combien coûte le ticket pour...?
kon'byañ koot luh tee'kay poor

What time is the last bus / train to...?
A quelle heure passe le dernier bus / train pour...?
a kel uhr pass luh dehr'nyay boos / trañ poor

BY SEA

Where do I catch the ferry to...?
Où est-ce que je peux prendre le ferry pour...?
oo ess kuh zhuh puh proñdr luh ferry poor

When does the next ferry / boat leave for...?

A quelle heure part le prochain ferry / bâteau pour...?

a kel uhr par luh pro'shañ ferry / ba'toh poor

Possible responses

It costs...

Cela coûte...

suh'la koot...

on the left / right

à gauche / à droite

a gohsh / a drwat

straight ahead
droit devant / tout droit
drwa duh'voñ / too drwa

over there
par là
par la

up / down the stairs
en haut / en bas des escaliers
oñ oh / oñ bah dayz esk'ally'ay

It will cost...euros per day / per week.
**Cela vous coûtera...euros par jour /
par semaine.**
*suh'la voo koot'uh'ra...uh'roh par
zhoor / par suh'men*

Follow the signs above.
Suivez les panneaux.
swee'vay lay pann'oh

There's a train to...at...
Il y a un train pour...à...heures.
eel ee a uñ trañ poor...a...uhr

Your train leaves from platform number...
Votre train part du quai numéro...
vo'tr trañ par doo kay noo'may'roh

You'll need bus number...for...
Il faut prendre le bus numéro... pour...
eel foh proñdr luh boos noo'may'roh...poor...

The next boat for...will leave at...
Le prochain bâteau pour...part à...heures.
luh pro'shañ ba'toh poor...par a...uhr

BEDS & BREAKFAST

HOTELS & HOSTELS

Do you have any vacancies?
Est-ce que vous avez des chambres libres?
ess kuh vooz av'ay day shoñbr leebr

I would like...
Je voudrais...
zhuh voo'dray

I reserved a single room / double room...
J'ai réservé une chambre simple / double...
zhay ray'zehr'vay oon shoñbr sañ'pl / doo'bl

with twin beds
avec deux lits
a'vek duh lee

with a double bed
avec un lit double
a'vek uñ lee doo'bl

with a shower and toilet
avec une douche et des toilettes
a'vek oon doosh ay day twa'let

with a bath
avec une baignoire
a'vek oon ben'war

How much is...?
Combien coûtent...? (plural)
koñ'byañ koot

bed and breakfast...
la chambre et le petit déjeuner...
la shoñbr ay luh puh'tee
  day'zhuh'nay

half-board...
la demi pension...
la duh'mee poñ'syoñ

full-board...
la pension complète
la poñ'syoñ koñ'plet

...per night
...par nuit
...par nwee

...per week
...par semaine
...par suh'men

I'd like to stay for...
Je voudrais rester pour...
zhuh voo'dray rest'ay poor

one night / two nights
une nuit / deux nuits
oon nwee / duh nwee

a week / two weeks
une semaine / deux semaines
oon suh'men / duh suh'men

Is there a reduction for children?
Y-a-t-il un tarif réduit pour les enfants?
*ee a teel uñ ta'reef ray'dwee poor layz
 oñ'foñ*

Do you have any cheaper rooms?
Avez-vous des chambres moins chères?
av'ay voo day shoñbr mwañ shehr

Does the room have...?
Est-ce que la chambre a...?
ess kuh la shoñbr

a radio / a television
une radio / une télévision
oon rad'ee'oh / oon te'le'vizy'oñ

room service
service d'étage
sehr'veess day'tazh

a mini-bar
un mini-bar
uñ mee'nee-bar

air-conditioning
la climatisation
la klee'ma'tee'zas'yoñ

a hairdryer
un séche cheveux
uñ sesh shuh'vuh

Is there a night-porter on duty?
Y-a-t-il un portier de nuit en service?
*ee a teel uñ port'ee'ay duh nwee oñ
    sehr'veess*

Can I have a wake-up call at...?
**Pouvez-vous me réveiller par téléphone
à...heure?**
*poo'vay voo muh ray'vay'ay par te'le'fon
    a...uhr*

I like to stay out late, so will I need a key?
**J'aime rester dehors tard, alors est-ce
que j'ai besoin d'une clé?**
*zhem rest'ay duh'or tar al'or ess kuh
    zhay buhz'wañ doon klay*

I'd like breakfast in my room tomorrow.
Je voudrais prendre mon petit-déjeuner dans ma chambre demain.
zhuh voo'dray proñdr moñ puh'tee day'zhuh'nay doñ ma shoñbr duh'mañ

What time is breakfast / dinner served?
A quelle heure est servi le petit-déjeuner / le dîner?
a kel uhr ay sehr'vee luh puh'tee day'zhuh'nay / luh dee'nay

The room is too cold / hot / small / dirty.
La chambre est trop froide / chaude / petite / sale.
la shoñbr ay troh fwod / shohde / puh'teet / sal

Could I have some clean towels, please?
Est-ce que je peux avoir des serviettes propres, s'il vous plaît?
ess kuh zhuh puhz av'war day sehr'vyet propr seel voo play

The shower doesn't work.
La douche ne marche pas.
la doosh nuh marsh pa.

I'm not satisfied and I'd like another room, please.
Je ne suis par satisfé et je voudrais une autre chambre, s'il vous plaît.
zhuh nuh swee pa sat'iss'fay ay zhuh voo'dray oon otr shoñbr, seel voo play

Can you recommend any good bars /
restaurants / night-clubs?

**Pouvez vous me recommander des bars /
des restaurants / des boîtes de nuit
sympathiques?**

*poo'vay voo muh ruh'kuh'moñ'day day bar
/ day restaurant / day bwa'te duh nwee
sam'pa'teek*

Are there any areas I should avoid at
night?

**Y a t'il des quartiers que je devrais éviter
la nuit?**

*ee a teel day karty'ay kuh zhuh duh'vray
ay'vee'tay la nwee*

I'd like to make a phone call.

Je voudrais passer un coup de fil.

zhuh voo'dray pass'ay uñ koo duh fee

Can I have my bill?
Est-ce que je peux avoir l'addition?
ess kuh zhuh puhz av'war la'dees'yoñ

CAMPING

Where's the nearest campsite?
Où est le camping le plus proche?
oo ay luh koñ'peeng luh ploo prosh

May we camp here?
Pouvons-nous camper ici?
poo'voñ noo koñ'pay ee'see

How much to stay here...?
Combien cela coûterait-t'il de rester ici...?
koñ'byañ suh'la koot'uh'ray teel duh res'tay ee'see

per day
par jour
par zhoor

per person
par personne
par pehr'son

per car
par voiture
par vwa'toor

per tent
par tente
par tahnt

per caravan
par caravane
par caravan

Where are the toilets / the showers?
Où sont les toilettes / les douches?
oo soñ lay twa'let / lay doosh

Are there / is there...?
Y-a-t-il...?
ee a teel

public telephones
des téléphones publiques
day te'le'fon poo'bleek

local shops
des magasins de quartier
day mag'azañ duh karty'ay

a swimming pool
une piscine
oon pee'seen

an electricity supply
une prise électrique
oon preez ay'layk'treek

Where's the nearest beach?
Où est la plage la plus proche?
oo ay la plazh la ploo prosh

Possible responses

We have no vacancies at the moment.
C'est complet en ce moment.
say koñ'play oñ se mo'moñ

I can recommend another hotel nearby.
Je peux vous recommander un autre hôtel près d'ici.
zhuh puh voo ruh'kuh'moñ'day uñ otr o'tel pray dee'see

How long do you want to stay?
Combien de temps voulez-vous rester?
koñ'byañ duh toñ voo'lay voo res'tay

It's half-price for children.
C'est demi tarif pour les enfants.
say duh'mee ta'reef poor layz oñ'foñ

There are no discounts for children.
Il n'y a pas de réductions pour les enfants.
eel nee a pa duh ray'dooks'yon poor layz oñ'foñ

That'll be...euros.
Cela fera...euros.
suh'la fuh'ra...uh'roh

MONEY, MONEY, MONEY

GETTING IT

Where can I find a...?
Où est-ce que je peux trouver...?
oo ess kuh zhuh puh troo'vay

> bank
> **une banque**
> *oon boñk*

currency exchange office
un bureau de change
uñ boo'roh duh shoñzh

cash machine
un distributeur
uñ dees'tree'boo'tuhr

What's the current exchange rate?
Quel est le taux de change actuel?
kel ay luh toh duh shoñzh ak'too'el

How much commission do you charge?
A combien s'élève la commission?
a koñ'byañ say'lev la komm'i'syoñ

I'd like to exchange these traveller's cheques / pounds for euros.
Je voudrais échanger ces chèques de voyage / livres contre des euros.
zhuh voo'dray ay'shoñ'zhay say shek duh vwa'yazh / leevr koñtr dayz uh'roh

SPENDING IT

How much is it?
C'est combien?
say koñ'byañ

Can I pay by credit card?
Est-ce que je peux payer par carte de crédit?
ess kuh zhuh puh pay'ay par kart duh kray'dee

Do you accept traveller's cheques?
Acceptez-vous les chèques de voyage?
ak'sep'tay voo lay shek duh vwa'yazh

FOOD, GLORIOUS FOOD

EATING OUT

Waiter / Waitress!
Serveur / Serveuse!
sehr'vuhr / sehr'vuhz

I'd like a table for one person / two people.
Je voudrais une table pour une personne / deux personnes.
zhuh voo'dray oon tabl poor oon pehr'son / duh pehr'son

Could we have a table...?
Pourrions-nous avoir une table...?
poo'ree'oñ nooz av'war oon tabl

in the corner
dans le coin
doñ luh kwañ

by the window
à côté de la fenêtre
a ko'tay duh la fuh'netr

outside
dehors
duh'or

in the smoking area
dans la zone fumeur
doñ la zon foo'muhr

in the non-smoking area
dans la zone non-fumeur
doñ la zon noñ-foo'muhr

Could we see the drinks / food menu?
Pourrions-nous avoir la carte des boissons / le menu?
poo'ree'oñ noo av'war la kart day bwa'soñ / luh muh'noo

I'd like to order some drinks, please.
Je voudrais commander des boissons, s'il vous plaît.
zhuh voo'dray ko'moñ'day day bwa'soñ seel voo play

I'd like...
Je voudrais...
zhuh voo'dray

a bottle of...
une bouteille de...
oon boo'tay duh

a glass / two glasses of...
un verre / deux verres de...
un vehr / duh vehr duh

46

red wine
vin rouge
vañ roozh

white wine
vin blanc
vañ bloñ

sparkling mineral water
de l'eau gazeuse
duh loh gaz'uhz

still mineral water
de l'eau minérale
duh loh mee'ne'ral

beer
la bière
la byehr

lager
la bière blonde
la byehr blond

cider
le cidre
luh see'dr

lemonade
limonade
lee'mon'ard

cola
coca
ko'ka

orange juice
jus d'orange
zhoo dor'anzh

apple juice
jus de pomme
zhoo duh pom

Do you have a children's menu?
Avez-vous un menu pour les enfants?
av'ay voo uñ muh'noo poor layz oñ'foñ

I'm a vegetarian. What do you
recommend?
**Je suis végétarien(ne). Qu'est-ce que
vous me recommandez?**
*zhuh swee ve'zhe'tar'yan(yen). kess kuh
voo muh ruh'ko'moñ'day*

Does this dish contain nuts / wheat?
**Est-ce que ce plat contient des noix /
du blé?**
*ess kuh suh pla koñ'tyañ day nwa /
doo blay*

I'd like to order...followed by...
Je voudrais commander...suivi de...
zhuh voo'dray ko'moñ'day...swee'vee duh

Could I see the dessert menu?
Est-ce que je peux voir la carte des desserts?
ess kuh zhuh puh vwar la kart day day'sehr

That was delicious. Thank you.
C'était délicieux. Merci.
say'tay day'lee'syuh. mehr'see

Can we order some coffee, please?
Est-ce que nous pouvons commander du café, s'il vous plaît?
ess kuh noo poo'voñ co'moñ'day doo ka'fay, seel voo play

(Could we have) the bill, please?
L'addition, s'il vous plaît?
la'dees'yoñ, seel voo play

Is service included?
Est-ce que le service est compris?
ess kuh luh sehr'veess ay coñ'pree

There's been a mistake. I didn't order that drink / meal.
Il y a eu une érreur. Je n'ai pas commandé cette boisson / ce repas.
eel ee a oo oon err'uhr. zhuh nay pa ko'moñ'day set bwa'soñ / suh ruh'pa

Possible responses

May I take your order?
Est-ce que je peux prendre votre commande?
ess kuh zhuh puh proñdr votr ko'moñ'd

I'd recommend...
Je recommande...
zhuh ruh'ko'moñd

Would you like...
Voudriez-vous...
voo'dree'ay voo

Enjoy your meal.
Bon appétit.
bon ap'e'tee

SIGHTS & SOUNDS

ATTRACTIONS & DIRECTIONS

Where is / Where are the...?
Où est / où sont les...?
oo ay / oo soñ lay

I'm lost. How do I get to the...?
Je me suis perdu(e). Comment est-ce que je fais pour aller à...?
zhuh muh swee pehr'doo. ko'moñt ess kuh zhuh fay poor all'ay a

airport
l'aéroport
la'ehr'o'por

art gallery
la gallerie d'art
la gal'e'ree dar

beach
la plage
la plazh

bus station
la gare routière
la gar root'yehr

castle
le château
luh sha'toh

cathedral
la cathédrale
la ka'tay'dral

cinema
le cinéma
luh see'nay'ma

harbour
le port
luh por

lake
le lac
luh lak

museum
le musée
luh moo'zay

park
le parc
luh park

river
la rivière
la ri'vee'yehr

stadium
le stade
luh stad

theatre
le théâtre
luh tay'atr

tourist information office
l'office du tourisme
loff'eess doo too'rees'm

town centre
le centre ville
luh soñtr veel

train station
la gare
la gar

zoo
le zoo
luh zoo

When does it open / close?
Ça ouvre / ferme à quelle heure?
sa oovr / fehrm a kel uhr

Is there an entrance fee?
Est-ce qu'il faut payer l'entrée?
ess keel foh pay'ay lañ'tray

Possible responses

Take the first / second / third turning
    on the left / right.
**Prenez la première / deuxième /
    troisième rue à gauche / droite.**
*pruh'nay la pruhm'yehr / duhz'yem /
    trwas'yem roo a gohsh / drwat*

Go straight on.
Allez tout droit.
all'ay too drwa

Around the corner.
C'est au coin de la rue.
say oh kwañ duh la roo

Along the street / road / avenue.
Le long de cette rue / route / avenue.
luh loñ duh set roo / root / av'en'oo

Over the bridge.
Traversez le pont.
tra'vehr'say luh poñ

It's a ten-minute walk down that road.
**C'est à dix minutes de marche par
  cette route.**
*say a dee mee'noot duh marsh par set
  root*

SPEND, SPEND, SPEND

SHOPPING

OPEN
Ouvert
oo'vehr

CLOSED
Fermé
fehr'may

ENTRANCE
Entrée
añ'tray

EXIT
Sortie
sor'tee

Where's the main shopping centre?
Où est le principal centre commercial?
oo ay luh prañ'see'pal señtr kom'ehr'see'al

Where can I find a...?
Où est-ce que je peux trouver...?
oo ess kuh zhuh puh troo'veh

baker's
la boulangerie
la boo'loñzh'uh'ree

bank
la banque
la boñk

bookshop
la librairie
la lee'bray'ree

butcher's
le boucher
luh boo'shay

chemist's
la pharmacie
la far'ma'see

clothes shop
le magasin de vêtements
luh mag'uh'zañ duh vehte'moñ

delicatessen
le traiteur
luh tray'tuhr

department store
le grand magasin
luh grañ mag'uh'zañ

fishmonger's
le poissonnier
luh pwa'sson'yay

gift shop
le magasin de cadeaux
luh mag'uh'zañ duh ka'doh

greengrocer's
l'épicerie
lay'pee'suh'ree

newsagent's
la presse
la press

post office
la poste
la posst

shoe shop
le magasin de chaussures
luh mag'uh'zañ duh shoh'ssoor

supermarket
le supermarché
luh soo'pehr'marsh'ay

wine merchant
le marchant de vin
luh marsh' oñ duh vañ

How much is it?
Combien ça coûte?
koñ'byañ sa koot

Excuse me, do you sell...?
Excusez moi, vendez-vous...?
eks'koo'zay mwa voñ'day voo

aspirin
de l'aspirine
duh lasp'ee'reen

camera films
des pellicules
day pe'lee'kool

cigarettes
des cigarettes
day sig'a'rett

condoms
des préservatifs
day pray'sehr'va'teef

English newspapers
des journaux anglais
day zhoor'noh oñ'glay

postcards
des cartes postales
day kart pos'tal

stamps
des timbres
day tañbr

street maps of the local area
des plans des alentours
day ploñ dayz al'oñ'toor

I'll take one / two / three of those.
Je vais en prendre un / deux / trois.
zhuh vayz oñ proñdr uñ / duh / trwa

I'll take it.
Je vais le prendre.
zhuh vay luh proñdr

That's too expensive. Do you have anything cheaper?

C'est trop cher. Avez-vous quelque chose de moins cher?

say troh shehr. a'vay voo kel'kuh shohz duh mwañ shehr

Where do I pay?

Où est-ce que je peux payer?

oo ess kuh zhuh puh pay'ay

Could I have a bag, please?

Est-ce que je peux avoir un sac, s'il vous plaît?

ess kuh zhuh puh av'war uñ sak seel voo play

Possible responses

Can I help you?
Est-ce que je peux vous aider?
ess kuh zhuh puh vooz ay'day

We don't sell...
Nous ne vendons pas de...
noo nuh voñ'doñ pa duh...

You can pay over there.
Vous pouvez payer là bas.
voo poo'vay pay'ay la ba

That'll be...euros, please.
Cela vous fera...euros, s'il vous plaît.
suh'la voo fuh'ra...ur'roh seel voo play

MEETING & GREETING

MAKING FRIENDS

Hi! My name's...
Salut! Je m'appelle...
sa'loo. zhuh ma'pel...

Pleased to meet you.
Heureux(se) de faire ta / votre connaissance.
uhr'ruh(ruhze) duh fehr ta / votr kon'ay'soñs

What's your name?
Comment vous appelez-vous?
ko'mon vooz ap'lay voo

Where are you from?
D'où venez-vous?
doo vuh'nay voo

I'm from England.
Je viens d'Angleterre.
zhuh vy'añ dañ'gluh'tehr

How are you doing?
Comment allez-vous?
ko'moñ tall'ay voo

Fine, thanks. And you?
Bien, merci. Et vous?
byañ mehr'see. ay voo

What do you do? [employment]
Que faites-vous dans la vie?
kuh feht voo doñ la vee

Would you like a drink?
Voudriez-vous boire quelque chose?
voo'dree'ay voo bwar kel'kuh shohz

Two beers, please.
Deux bières, s'il vous plaît.
duh byehr seel voo play

My friend is paying.
C'est mon ami qui paye.
say mon am'ee kee pay

What's your friend's name?
Comment s'appelle votre ami(e)?
ko'moñ sa'pel votr am'ee

Are you single / married?
Etes-vous célibataire / marié(e)?
et voo say'lee'ba'tehr / mar'ee'ay

Are you waiting for someone?
Attendez-vous quelqu'un?
at'oñ'day voo kel'kun

Do you want to dance?
Voulez-vous dancer?
voo'lay voo doñ'say

You're a great dancer!
Vous dansez très bien!
voo doñ'say tray byañ

Would you like to have dinner with me?
Voulez-vous dîner avec moi?
voo'lay voo dee'nay a'vek mwa

Can I have your phone number / e-mail address?
Pourrais-je avoir votre numéro de téléphone / adresse e-mail?
poo'rayzh av'war votr noo'may'roh duh te'le'fon / ad'ress ee'mayl

Here's my phone number. Call me some time.
Voici mon numéro de téléphone.
  Appelez-moi à l'occasion.
vwa'see moñ noo'may'roh duh te'le'fon.
  ap'lay mwa a lo'ka'zyon

Can I see you again tomorrow?
Est-ce que je peux vous revoir demain?
ess kuh zhuh puh voo ruh'vwar duh'mañ

Possible responses

I'd love to, thanks.
Cela me ferait très plaisir, merci.
*suh'la muh fuh'ray tray play'zeer
mehr'see*

I have a boyfriend / girlfriend back home.
**J'ai un petit ami / une petite amie chez
moi.**
*zhay uñ puh'tee am'ee / oon puh'teet
am'ee shay mwa*

Sorry, I'm with someone.
Desolé(e), je suis avec quelqu'un.
day'zo'lay zhuh sweez a'vek kel'kuñ

I've had a great evening.
J'ai passé une soirée très agréable.
*zhay pass'ay oon swa'ray trayz
  ag'ray'arbl*

Leave me alone.
Laissez moi tranquil(le).
less'ay mwa troñ'kee(keel)

Sorry, you're not my type.
Desolé(e), vous n'êtes pas mon type.
day'zo'lay voo net pa moñ teep

EMERGENCIES

Call the police!
Appelez la police!
ap'lay la poh'leess

My purse / wallet / bag / passport /
mobile phone has been stolen.
**Mon porte-monnaie / portefeuille /
sac / passeport / téléphone portable
a été volé.**
*moñ port'mon'ay / port'foy / sak /
pass'por / te'le'fon port'abl a ay'tay vol'ay*

Stop thief!
Au voleur!
oh vol'uhr

Where's the police station?
Où est le commissariat?
oo ay luh kom'ee'sa'ree'a

Look out!
Attention!
a'toñ'syoñ

Fire!
Au feu!
oh fuh

Where's the emergency exit?
Où est l'issue de secours?
oo ay liss'oo duh suh'koor

Where's the hospital?
Où est l'hôpital?
oo ay lop'ee'tal

I feel ill.
Je me sens malade.
zhuh muh soñ mal'ard

I'm going to be sick.
Je vais vomir.
zhuh vay vo'meer

I've a terrible headache.
J'ai un terrible mal de tête.
zhay uñ te'reebl mal duh tet

It hurts here...[point].
Ça me fait mal ici.
sa muh fay mal ee'see

Please call for a doctor / ambulance.
**Appelez un docteur / une ambulance,
s'il vous plaît.**
*ap'lay uñ dok'tuhr / oon oñ'boo'loñss
seel voo play*

I'm taking this prescription medication.
**Je prends ce médicament sur
préscription.**
*zhuh proñ suh may'dee'ka'moñ soor
pray'scryp'syon*

I'm pregnant.
Je suis enceinte.
zhuh sweez on'sañt

Help!
A l'aide!
a layd

I'm lost. Can you help me?
Je me suis perdu(e). Pouvez-vous m'aider?
zhuh muh swee pehr'doo. poo'vay voo may'day

REFERENCE

NUMBERS

0 zero
zéro
ze'ro

1 one
un
uñ

2 two
deux
duh

3 three
trois
trwa

4 four
quatre
katr

5 five
cinq
sañk

6	six	10	ten
	six		**dix**
	seess		*deess*

7	seven	11	eleven
	sept		**onze**
	set		*oñz*

8	eight	12	twelve
	huit		**douze**
	weet		*dooz*

9	nine	13	thirteen
	neuf		**treize**
	nuhf		*trez*

14 fourteen
quatorze
ka'torz

18 eighteen
dix-huit
dees'weet

15 fifteen
quinze
kañz

19 nineteen
dix-neuf
dees'nuhf

16 sixteen
seize
sez

20 twenty
vingt
vañ

17 seventeen
dix-sept
dees'set

21 twenty-one
vingt et un
vañt'ay'uñ

22 twenty-two
vingt-deux
vañ'duh

30 thirty
trente
troñt

31 thirty-one
trente et un
troñt'ay'uñ

32 thirty-two
trente-deux
troñt'duh

40 forty
quarante
ka'roñt

60 sixty
soixante
swa'soñt

41 forty-one
quarante et un
ka'ront'ay'uñ

70 seventy
soixante-dix
swa'soñt'deess

42 forty-two
quarante-deux
ka'roñt'duh

80 eighty
quatre-vingts
katr'vañ

50 fifty
cinquante
sañ'koñt

90 ninety
quatre-vingt-dix
katr'vañ'deess

100 one hundred **cent** *soñ*	**1,000** one thousand **mille** *meel*
101 one hundred and one **cent et un** *soñt'ay'uñ*	**5,000** five thousand **cinq mille** *sañk meel*
150 one hundred and fifty **cent-cinquante** *soñ sañ'koñt*	**1,000,000** one million **un million** *uñ meel'yoñ*
200 two hundred **deux cents** *duh soñ*	

DAYS OF THE WEEK

Monday
lundi
luñ'dee

Friday
vendredi
voñ'druh'dee

Tuesday
mardi
mar'dee

Saturday
samedi
sam'dee

Wednesday
mercredi
mehr'kruh'dee

Sunday
dimanche
dee'moñsh

Thursday
jeudi
zhuh'dee

MONTHS OF THE YEAR

January
janvier
zhoñ'vee'ay

May
mai
may

February
février
fay'vree'ay

June
juin
zhoo'añ

March
mars
marss

July
juillet
zhoo'ee'ay

April
avril
a'vreel

August
août
oo

September
septembre
sep'toñbr

October
octobre
oc'tobr

November
novembre
noh'voñbr

December
décembre
day'soñbr

TIMES OF DAY

today
aujourd'hui
oh'zhoor'dwee

afternoon
l'apres-midi
lap'ray mee'dee

tomorrow
demain
duh'mañ

evening
le soir
luh swar

yesterday
hier
ee'ehr

now
maintenant
mañ'te'noñ

morning
le matin
luh ma'tañ

later
plus tard
ploo tar

TIME

Excuse me. What's the time?
Excusez-moi. Quelle heure est-il?
eks'koo'zay mwa. kel uhr ay'teel

It's one o'clock.
Il est une heure.
eel ayt oon uhr

It's quarter to eight.
Il est huit heure moins le quart.
eel ay weet uhr mwoñ luh kar

It's half past two.
Il est deux heure et demi.
eel ay duhz uhr ay duh'mee

It's quarter past ten.
Il est dix heure et quart.
eel ay deez uhr ay kar

Five past seven.
Sept heure cinq.
set uhr sañk

Ten past eleven.
Onze heure dix.
oñz uhr deess

Ten to five.
Cinq heure moins dix.
sañk uhr mwoñ deess

Twelve o'clock (noon / midnight)
Midi / Minuit
mee'dee / mee'nwee